# Goodness
# Kindness
# And Love

## Selected Poetry

## Shakil A l Dawood

Shakil Ahmed Ismail Dawood began writing poetry just over twenty years ago, and has published several volumes of poetry to date.

He feels that poetry ought to, as a main thesis, narrate the reality of human beings, and the greatest reality of humans is their propensity for virtue, for every manifestation of goodness, kindness and love.

He is versed in Biochemistry, Environmental Studies, Geography and psychotherapy. His other interests are the written word, classical music and visual Art.

Copyright © Shakil A. I. Dawood.
September 2014, LONDON.

Cover Painting:
"Diptych" by Colin Selley.

# AN INTRODUCTORY NOTE.

Welcome to another edition of the 'Aspects of the Heart' series. This book finds me let loose and roaming randomly in the vast expanse of the heart.

And the heart being the seat and conduit of courage, goodness, kindness and Love, it is necessary that I have devoted this poetry almost exclusively to these human virtues.

It is high time that what is precious and salutary about the human being was celebrated: we live in dark times: the good, kind and loving person in this darkness stands out like a beacon or lighthouse.

It is to celebrate the beauty of human luminescence that I have selected these poems, as it turned out, randomly from those I had at hand.

The least goodness is worth its weight in gold; and whatever goodness weighs an ounce, the poet must make it into a pound.

If people could only recognize the inestimable value of a smile or a 'Good morning', then moments of goodness, kindness and Love would be the crowning glory of human experience.

And this is my aim in this volume of verse: to enable people to fully and sincerely gauge and understand virtue, and place it at the apex of what is humanly possible.

Copyright © Shakil Ahmed Ismail Dawood, September, 2014 London.

A little child is more accomplished and more important than a martyr. Last month, August 2014, a little baby girl was born to my niece, Naazneen. She was called Nusaybah.

This book is dedicated to this grandniece and every little child in the world like her: the finest, most majestic and greatest resource humanity has ever possessed.

# Goodness Kindness and Love

# THE POEMS

# **BECOMING BEAUTIFUL OR HANDSOME**

You smile,
And exchange a greeting –
What a manifestly immense world
You are immersing yourself in;

The vast universe
Of spiritual majesty –
Of real, true human feeling and motion;

With your smile and greeting,
You have introduced yourself to,
And ushered yourself into
This great, incomparable expanse,
And in the finest manner
Have enlarged and magnified
Its already immense range and scope –

Your goodness
Has extended the beauty
Of the inner world of humanity.

And your smile and greeting
has taken me,
And introduced me
To this huge beautiful dimension,
Widening the bounds
Of my own great inward territory
and realm:

The meaning of the least goodness
Thus is the expansion and deepening
Of the experiencing universe of
individuals,
The experience of the celestial
and sublime,
The making of sacrosanct individuals,
Sovereign people who are partaking of
that goodness,
As I did, when you smiled at me
And greeted me!

How wise is it then,
To decide to smile at somebody,
Or greet her or him?

# **THE CROWNING OF ONESELF........**

In a stream,
I feel your humanity –
And perhaps your heart and soul,
Destined to suffer and feel pain.

All of us are fated to undergo difficulties
When you are occupied with your trial
in mind and heart,
You are journeying beyond,
transcending –
For you are being compounded,
concentrated
Into distilled substance significant
and rich;

You are now qualified to take a real
view of the world,
And possess the stature
By which you are heeded by the world;

The night at its darkest point,
Is replete with the bright lamp of dawn,

And to be wise is not far from
those who suffer —
Their very virtue is great wisdom;

And in all this,
your humanity does not budge,
And remains the mainstay
of your makeup,
And you, suffering,
Are transforming the considerable jewel
of your humanity
Into your crown;

The best coronation,
The most magnificent crowning
Is by one's own self,
When we maintain our humanity
Despite tribulation;

Your humanity,
Your goodness,
Now becomes powerful,
Forceful,
And you can be categorized

A real sovereign and monarch
in the world.

And then, in a stream,
I again feel your humanity,
The brightest lamp!
And there is no blemish in you;

Your faults have been masked
by your adjudication-
Of your trial with your humanity
and goodness
And your good thought;

And the day of your existence
Has yet barely dawned for you,
How great will you become today,
The next day and the next?
How sublime is your potential?

If your life is the day,
In the night
Your tremendous qualities will mature
And beautify more meaningfully –

For, loss has left you,
And when detached,
Your humanity can only gain interest!


## **'A BEAUTIFUL VISION COMPLETE.'**

A beautiful vision complete –
Filling my dreams wholly, replete –

I took one sip from the offered goblet,
And am totally drunk, without regret –

What is this 'complete' beautiful vision?
It is my most ardent, greatest mission –

To discover one kind,
caring and sympathetic:
I did – and Love's wine was
viscous and thick,

Rich with possibilities of Love,
this one is truly great,
Great, if only for a moment her or him
feeling this state;

And I am lovingly ushered
away from my turmoil –
This witnessing of kindness,
of foils is the perfect foil;

For impasse, tragedy,
tribulation and grief,
Replacing my blood,
this is heart's instant relief –

Who is this 'beautiful vision complete'?
*Kind you, who does
my predicament unseat;*
You handsome or beautiful,
are a being rare:
Nobody like you – you're unique
and you share!

Monday, 28/10/2013, 10.36 p.m.

# **A BIRTHDAY POEM FOR YOU...**

*And now, you are a year older, growing older, together with all the changes the passage of year cause to nature and to you........*

The moon waxes and wanes;
The seasons change;

Flowers bloom and wither;
The ocean exhales and inhales;

The rivers change position;
They relentlessly pursue the sea;

Day stalks night and
night transforms into day;

The stars blink, one moment
lamp-like, the next dark;

Some baby animals grow
into precious adults;

Lack of knowledge
turns into intelligence,

And intelligence becomes wisdom;
Indifference slides into virtuous
behaviour;

Everything good is moving, dynamic,
Over the course of the
passage of a year,

Save one great thing,
which remains exactly the same,
And is the same perpetually and
forever:

And that is the accomplishment
of your beauty!

## **A BLADE OF GRASS....**

A blade of grass
Is easily dismissed, as ordinary, negligible
However, what is its stature
and greatness
If the eye of a human being
falls upon it?

The human being, with his
or her one glance
Transmits, and trans-locates their entire
being to that blade of grass –
They impart their learning, culture, Art,
science, divinity, wisdom;

Their entire being and humanity
To it, transforming it, making it a
massive volume, infinite in nature
and greatly valuable –

Hence, next time you see a blade of
grass, remember that
A man,
A woman,
A nurse, a good mother, a kind father,
a teacher, a saint
Has looked upon it, making it priceless;
Remember that God too, is always
looking at that blade of grass;

Spare another thought,
however, for that single leaf
of incalculably rich grass –
What if a little child smiled at it,
As children are wont to
do to things of nature-
Would it not then,
be much more so beyond value?


Tuesday, 24/09/2013, 7.35 p.m.

## AN EID AND CHRISTMAS THOUGHT FOR YOU LITTLE CHILD.........

For Eid or Christmas
I patiently wait –
Because they are a
Special date.

For me to exercise
Great selection –
For the toys I choose,
Are for you my affection!

It is voluntary love
That thus impels me,
And this love, great,
Is with me constantly.

So constant is this love
In my life and living,
I can only reciprocate
Adequately by giving!

Little children, given to the
world by God,
Make me man's shepherd:
my love my rod!

Love and best wishes,
For the very special little children,
Let it be a very special Eid or Christmas
And a very special New Year!

# A DEFINITION OF 'BEAUTIFUL'....

The most powerful and greatest
occurrences and designs
In the human being are
in his or her heart –
These are respect and Love;

These virtues do not have to be earned
By any recipient individual in the world

The generous heart will respect and
Love unconditionally,
Even when this respect and
Love is not deserved;

However, there is a great person
That fully deserves every compliment
and virtue the great heart can
afford and bestow –

One that naturally draws out voluntary
respect and Love-

And this is the beautiful human being –
True human beings – little children,
good mothers, virtuous fathers,
kind persons;

Are examples of beautiful humans,
And can be defined as such –
This is a true human being,
And as we say, true human beings are
by very definition, beautiful:

The human tongue can speak
myriad languages,
Yet the most eloquent words are those
that confirm an individual as a *true*
human being: comforting words:

Kind words –
That is, beautiful speech
at its most beauteous –
And the one who deserves
it is truly most beautiful;

Human thinking conjures up a
well of inspired imaginative images;

Yet the one that visualizes kindness
in thought, word, and deed
Is the most imaginative possible
to the human being –

Being the height of the imagination,
it is beautiful;

Human actions can vary in impression,
But the ones that follow practically,
kindness in intention
Are the finest and truly the most
beautiful...

The ones who practice the beautiful are
the beautiful!

Sunday, 15/07/2012, 7.56 p.m.

# **A DREAM FOR YOU………**

May you have huge strength –
And a strong, loving plan –
That extends and anchors
Throughout your life-span!

May you wholly, always, use
Your intellect and heart to the full –
May these towards you
Every honour and majesty pull!

May you amplify your heart
To its greatest extent
May every opportunity in using it,
From heaven condescend!

May your interactions be kind –
The best of relationships –
May these experiences be choice,
As the bee only the nectar sips!

May you be guided in life
By someone sage and wise,
May your every moment of giving
Be the finest enterprise!

May you possess surfeit Love
Enough for this entire existence,
May you be kind and loving
In every deed, every instance!

May your ambitions and desire
Be completely fulfilled
And may you help, enable the world
To be with kindness instilled!

And may Love, great Love beckon,
And this great Love you give,
And may the life you've been given
You to the hilt, to the fullest live!

Thursday, 26/06/2014, 10.10 p.m.

# **TO ADVANCE IN LIFE.**

*'We need the Vision true –
not what the world reveals ;
'We need that Meaning
which contention cannot yield.'*
( Yunus Emre )

To really, truly, advance in
life is to mature;

Real advancement is an inner
phenomenon,
When we realize that we have become
caring and kind;

The moment real and true maturity
Is realized and consolidated however
Is when we feel compassion,
For those who do us wrong—
When we treat cruelty with kindness:

Forgiveness is the key to
this brave action:
It is an untold advance in
a human being,
And the greatest possible success
for him or her;

Success is not so much acquiring a
formal education, Or wealth,
But it is the tendency to separate from
your need to retaliate,
And to transform your inner being such
that no man can become a foe,
And the cause of enmity is defeated.

Little children innately embody
this grand state:

How successful and great are little
children?

## A FACT: YOUR BEAUTY CANNOT BE TAKEN AWAY FROM YOU!

Your beauty cannot be
taken away from you,
Nor the imperative work
of that beauty:
Just as a flower blossoms only to heal,
You have blossomed into majestic
beauty simply to heal;
And this beauty lies in the heart –
The heart's great qualities:

It is the heart that heals.

Every person is born with a great heart,
as they have been born a child, and this
great heart always lies within, even in
adulthood.

Good intentions awaken your heart,
And implementing these through
speech or action is the healing –

If people only knew the tremendous
healing power inherent in the merest
good word or action;

They would embrace its actor, and be
forever grateful –
Thus, most people forsake the
opportunity to be healed,
Because they do not value the beauty
of the 'small' kind word or act.

Nonetheless, you by the mere
fact of your authentic beauty
are a true healer,
And this huge stature cannot be taken
away from you, by anything, or anyone:

Old age will not wither your fabulous
beauty,
Not will death diminish it:
You will be beautiful forever!

# A HUMAN BEING IS A FLOWER, A FLOWER IS A HUMAN BEING.

A flower, one day,
Is no more:
A love gone astray
Makes work your core:

A flower once,
Brought healing:
It brought balance
Without kneeling;

A love gone away,
Away forever,
Takes all into its sway,
And *seems* all to sever;

A flower is cause
For thought;
It is time to pause
And to *heart* be brought;

A flower always
Is at a premium –
"Be yourself," it says,
"And in all things medium."

A love gone far, far,
Is lost, is only lost
To one who does mar
The heart as perennial host;

A human flower
Will understand and see
With every power
And pay every fee:

A love unrequited
Is for the selected:
It isn't life blighted,
But Love detected!

Because a flower
Has clearly shown
That the hour
Is yours — your own!

So when love goes,
Let Love be moved
And so grief's throes
Are true Love proved!

Wednesday, 20/01/2010, 5.25 p.m.

## YOU ARE A JEWEL : A SUFFERING PERSON'S TESTIMONY.

*'The greatness of a person does not depend on their education, their wealth, or their physical beauty or handsomeness. It depends on their heart – if their heart is great, then they are great.'* MUHAMMAD ALI.

'Things that are immaterial, and taken from the unseen – like Art, human greatness, love, kindness and goodness are the greatest phenomenon in the universe.

More precious than gold or diamonds, they can help the sick person overcome his or her sickness.

Today, when I met you I was unwell.

Your lovely, unspoken presence – full of unspoken care and consideration; spoke yet again of the immensity of wealth in your inner, unseen world.

And in even the very brief conversation with me, you drew unconsciously on that vast and rich inner universe.

My being unwell was dispelled and I felt whole again.

It takes a jeweller to know the value of a diamond – to a non-jeweller it is a piece of glass.

I can say with certitude, without any arrogance, that my long suffering has qualified me to be a jeweller of the unseen world of people and I can really value their precious good words, thoughts and actions.

A doctor's medicine would not have saved me today; nor financial riches, nor mere physical beauty.

What saved me was your beauty, moulded and tempered by a lovely personality, with its intention of Goodness, Kindness and Love.

If your heart is beyond worldly wealth, and worldly education, and beyond mere physical beauty, how can a person like me describe the jewel you are?

What is the state of your heart and thus, your condition?

The answer is greatness!

# A KINDLY MEANT POEM FOR YOU, A GRACIOUS WOMAN.

Flowers, rooted in the soil are
*fated* to bloom into beauty;
You, rooted in the human world
since infancy;

*Chose* to blossom into a wonderful
human being;
Flowers exude healing through
tremendous beauty;

Your wonder is as greatly
comforting too –
You smile readily,
And are quick with a consoling word;

But, a flower only blooms once –
You blossom and flourish all the time;

Through your nobility,
You enable other individuals to blossom
Your kindness magnifies their souls

And brings them hope, paving their
way to positive action;

Your goodness sets people on the path
to victory – kindness – in life,
And simply by being what you are,
You are victorious yourself;

The wonder of kindness and goodness
Is the wonder of instantly
realized maturity,
And yet your nature matures
all the time;

A flower matures, and though
increasing in beauty,
It eventually withers –

And as you mature, you do
amplify in maturity, yes,
Added to the fact that you have,
by your beautiful conduct,
Blossomed once and forever!

# **THE LITTLE CHILD'S POEM......**

Little child, you are so tiny and helpless and only one –
Yet, yet against all worldly odds, you have certainly won!

For you have horses, flowers, oceans and Love been built,
And you are Beauty, power, influence and loving to the hilt!

God's Greatest Creation was your personality – your creation,
For your heart and mind has to the universe deep, intimate relation!

Though you are so tiny, seemingly helpless and seem feeble,
You have ascended to the summit – surmounting every steeple!

You are more beauty than beauty; your eyes are starrier than starry,

And God and His immense universe in
your great heart you carry!

You communicate naught but Love –
you're Love's impetuous jet,
In your greatness did God and the
universe rise: in it They will set!

You know no bounds, no unknowing,
no indifference, no prejudice,
Your thought is Love, your mind Love
and you are Love's justice!

You shirk nothing, courageous, and you
meet the world face to face,
Of everything in God's creation, it is you
that I want to embrace!

Little child of all human achieving, you
are greater: the greatest:
Love you are, Love you choose for the
world: for it Love manifest!

Tuesday 15/04/2014, 9.11 p.m.

## **LOVE..........**

Love
Is the greatest
Entity in the universe:

The purveyor of Love
Thus is intimate, With human
And celestial greatness:

To feel Love
Is sublime,
The finest feeling;

To give Love,
However, Is more pleasurable
Than receiving it –

How most unfortunate then,
Him or her, Who never give Love,
And how fortunate
And great then,
Those who do so?
           Sunday, 24/08/2014, 2.50 p.m.

## A POEM ABOUT YOUR DISREGARD AND IGNORANCE............

You have total disregard
For the inhumane,
The unkind,
And the unloving;

And you are, personally,
Absolutely ignorant
Of the inhumane attitude,
The unkind word
And the unloving action –

And, how great, how beautiful
Are you in this utter disregard,
And absolute ignorance!


Wednesday, 09/04/2014, 10.22 a.m.

## A POEM FOR A BELOVED............

My mind, my heart, my eyes
Stand ever-ready
To be ennobled and graced:

What I think, what I feel,
what I intend And what I see
Is prepared to be honoured and
emboldened –

My mind by your clear thought;
My heart by your profound
 goodness and kindness,
My aspirations enabled in noble design,
And my eyes by your great beauty –

What further, then becomes of my
mind, heart and eyes?

My mind becomes knowledgeable of
casting luminescence in the dark;
My heart becomes versed in forgiveness,
kindness and Love,

And my eyes no longer envision
ugliness-

And what happens to your mind, heart
and eyes in all this?

Your mind is your heart,
And your heart is your mind;
And your eyes prepare to witness what
your mind and heart aspire to and
desire:

Your mind becomes Love in action,
Your heart action in Love,
And your eyes perceive the
beautification of both –
Your mind and heart made great and
sublime!

And all my aspirations reach their
culmination –
They find and discover the surest guide
In your great and sublime personality!

## **A POEM FOR A DOG LOVER.....**

My dear friend,
You Love dogs –
Their love eases up pain
And clears the heart's fogs!

And they say that a dog
Is man's best friend –
That great Love it gives freely;
A dog – great – does not Love lend!

Your dog only has
Very good intentions –
Its qualities thus are
The best Divine inventions!

Your dog is the best
For its main emotional theme
Is to be supportive to you –
To the extreme!

Love your dog then
O fortunate pet owner –
Be kind to it, which of Love
Is finest donor!

                    Thursday, 11/09/2014, 2.54 p.m.

## A POEM FOR A GOOD HUMAN BEING.

Your grief and sorrow's depth
Is to magnify and deepen you;

Your thorns were made
As protection for beauty — the rose like;

You were born beautiful
To forever adorn creation;

Your personality is fashioned
Solely to beautify humanity and nature;

Your chosen, developed character exists
Only to usher greatness into the world;

Your mind's brilliance is limited
To intensify consideration and care for all;

Your heart works industriously, capaciously
To create — and give — Love;

Your constant resort to kindness is duly
To promote sanity around you;

Your life exists as a vast resource
To nobly supplement all life on earth;

The divine in you — the child and adult—

Enables this world to become a heaven:
Your soul exists in only one dimension:
As heavenly bliss in itself!

Sunday, 27/01/2013, 3.25 p.m.

# **A POEM FOR A GOOD MOTHER....**

When I am in the room with you,
dear Mother,
You are far away, like a star,
living deeply in the heavens,
Close companion of God
and conversing with angels;

And when I am in the room with you,
dear Mother,
You are so near, and have brought the
heavenly world to me;

If I look into your heart, there are all the
angels, praying for you,
The world of Love in your heart,
the world from which you draw your
great love for me and everybody else;

Your heart is your source of power, a
tremendous heart,
One that the angels prefer to live in,
rather than the heavens,

And in it the entire Love necessary to
Love not only your family,
But every particle in the universe,
that is the Love you have –
That is how much the universe
owes you;

What rank and status do you
have in this world then?
Your great worth cannot be
humanly calculated or computed;

And the angels are stretched in their
ability to calculate your stature,
as only God can compute that,
only He possesses the Vast Intellect to
analyse the meaning you are;

And you are already an inhabitant
of heaven –
That is God's least gesture towards you;

Towards a human being that has far
more meaning than even the angels;

What at the end of the day have you
shown the world, dear Mother?
The power of Love!

Mother, your Love is the most powerful
thing of any kind,
So luminous, it outshines the sun –
the sun it can make blind!

Mother, you always put me first, and
yourself always last,
Which is why you are wonderfully
in a heavenly mould cast!

Mother, you only desire peace
and Love for your child –
In this you're in every thought,
word and action reconciled!

Mother, to witness a heavenly being I
only need to see you,
So generous are you, you always give
everything you accrue!

Mother, all and everything do
I and the world owe you,
And neither can we repay you –
only God can that fact review!

Mother, I and the angels Love you:
we can only show you Love;
And you want nothing from angel
or child – nothing is enough!

Your Love – the Mother's Love;
is the strongest,
most enduring Love in existence,
No earthly reason can warrant such
inner strength and power,
The power of the qualities you possess,
Save a might drawn.
from the Unseen realms;

The realms from which the angels
draw their strength:
It is easier to say that angels draw their
strength from good Mothers!

## THE RISE OF THE DAWN

The dawn rises,
And the dusk falls,
Without fail,
Each day –

And the stars and moon
Come out And the heavens
Are glorified!

There is thus,
A beginning,
And an end
To each transacted day;

Human history
And existence
Is but nearly 'one day' old;

Do you not think,
Since this dark history
Has begun,
It at some time today,
Will end,
And the glory of heaven
Will be revealed?

Sunday, 24 / 08 / 2014, 3.03 p.m.

# **A POEM FOR A GREAT PERSON...**

To think, speak or act kindly is great anyway:
To be kind after a trial is infinitely greater!

Though at times reduced to a crescent,
The moon never fails to its duty
To be loveliness in our darkness,
In our night-time;

Though of a short duration,
And with a tantalizing, precarious longevity,
Flowers never fail, every spring,
In their duty to arrive at majestic healing –

Though sentenced to oblivion for half of each day,
Every single morning
The sun never fails in its duty
To bring light and warmth –

The moon, flowers and sun hence
Are the very stuff of natural greatness,
By overcoming, in such beautiful manner,
Their handicaps!

And you, a human being, are greater than
moon, flowers sun – anyway;
And waylaid by difficulty and sorrow,
You never fail in your duty of beautiful
charity of kindness to others.

You achieve the greatest beauty thus:
Through your duty of being kind.

Greater than moon, flowers
and sun, anyway,
Your difficulties and sorrow
Are the bejewelled wrapping around
an already golden existence –
your inherent quality of humanity;

Your pain is therefore the
making of you,
For to act kindly after tribulation
as you do;

Is the closest human beings can arrive at the
duties of the angelic, saintly, Prophetic and
the Divine;

The angels, saints, Prophets and God –
They who shimmer with genius and brilliance;

Hence the most beautiful, luminous state becomes yours,
And the greatest height belongs to you
In your duty of kindness,

Far and away beyond
The already great moon, flowers and sun!

To think, speak or act kindly is great enough anyway:
It is far greater still;
To do so after facing problems and difficulty!

Saturday, 02/11/2013, 9.38 p.m.

# **A POEM FOR A KIND FRIEND....**

All the languages of the entire world,
Are poor – poverty stricken,
When it comes to describing you;

All the great poets of the world,
Past and present
Are quiet restricted when describing you.

This is because every tongue
And every great poet
Has only one word – only one word:
To describe you
Appropriately and adequately;

It is 'beautiful' -

This is because you are kind
Which is a mixed collection,
Of all the tremendous and great qualities
That in total make you beautiful,
Truly beautiful,
And all the great poets,
And all the languages
Cannot ever describe the beautiful!

Therefore you are restricted to being
'beautiful'
By the most articulate people,
The poets —

But that which is truly restricted,
Like the moon confined to darkness,
Like a little child unable to look after itself —
Restricted like you —
Is the greatest beauty!

Monday, 28/03/2011, 6.39 p.m.
YMm

# **A POEM FOR A PERSON FACING TROUBLES......**

Your troubles – remorseless, endless, strong-in-themselves, to which
you seem irrevocably bound, held fast,
A trial that issues serious tribulations,
troubles hitherto not experienced,
dark depths hitherto unvisited:

And you seem without recourse, without option, your opinion   disregarded –
It is no cul-de-sac,
but a one-way journey and travel:
What can you do?

The sun belongs to you,
as do the moon and stars –
Their brilliance at your service;
The flowers' genius decidedly at the command of your needs – to live and die for you – and for you only:

Every flower that blooms on earth and every one that will bloom especially for your sake –

Every flower sees your personality and all
that befalls it as gain for itself,
an augmenting of its loveliness;

Your personality's loveliness has been, and is,
Your legacy of many smiles, greetings,
kind words and good actions,
And your positive intentions and impetus to
repeat the same;

Journeying headlong into the depths of
difficulty armed with your virtues –
a tremendous gift:

Space and time, which belong to you, to fill
with great thought,
good words and the finest actions;

Space and time, to use to read beautiful
books, glance at beautiful
Art, to utilize it fully, listening to beautiful
music,

To foster your immensely valuable inner
growth with the Love of animals and
nature;

To eat and drink wholesome;
To wear fresh clean clothes;

To be informal and comfortable in the company of the beautiful –

The good men and women and little children;
To show beautiful care for the elderly;
To think, meditate, to create beautiful artefacts:

And then, your crowning glory –
Loving little children and being loved by them in return!

Perhaps your agony was created that you possess a foil to existence;

That you truly appreciate and value
What is available to you in this world,
And its greatness and Beauty!

Sunday, 13/04/2014, 2.58 p.m.
YMm.

## **A POEM FOR A SMILING WOMAN.**

To smile
Is to commit a magnificent action –
A masterly and complete
Divine, spiritual, intellectual, emotional,
saintly and angelic act;

Because your smile is complete,
In every way,
It is an eternal action –
It lives on, forever –
Never to be obscured or diminished;

If your smile is an eternal action,
How much do you acquire eternity
Through your kindness and goodness?
And how immortal do you become
Through your Love?

And, how great is your heart?

Tuesday, 05/11/2013, 12.12 p.m.

# A POEM FOR A SPECIAL GIRL............

Attention to Love will every,
every great quality unfurl –
Because, our exclusive focus is you,
a very special girl;

You're special because you attend to your qualities:
Kindness, goodness and Love;
your beautiful abilities;

You, a special person,
see the good and kind as exalted:
And so you are: we Love you and by us
you're wanted;

You are special moreover,
because to all you're a friend,
To you our good wishes and my very special
Love I send:

My dear, never change –
remain the way you are:
You have come far in life:
in future you will go far!
      Friday, 27/05/2011, 6.11 p.m.

## A POEM FOR A TRUTHFUL WOMAN.

Waves of affliction and sorrow
Have trusted your heart to be their shore;
You have been liberally provided
with difficulty
And deprived of provisions
Against the stream of trials.

And yet, you smile,
Are constructive,
And are good to me and others.

Out of the pyre and ashes of your problems
You have arisen,
Blessed,
And have written an original page
On the real history of the world,
Which is about good thoughts,
words and deeds.

With little repose, you have guided yourself
To the authentic Truth –
And the Truth is *Goodness,
Kindness and Love.*

And brought, with your goodness,
Angels to the world.

What does your virtue and goodness
make you then,
In the eyes of the troubled world,
In the eyes of angels,
In the eyes of the saints and Prophets,
In the Eyes of God?

However, you are truly crowned
When a little child,
Sensing your goodness and Love
Instinctively and implicitly trusts you;

And willingly puts his or her hand in yours –
That is your eternal, immortal moment,
And your greatest achievement!

## **A POEM FOR YOU.**

The moon in darkness
Gives illumination –
Thus, in the dark,
It gives hope;

You, in my darkness,
Give me hope
With the treasure of your empathy
And good nature;

What is the relationship of the moon to you?

The moon is beauty exemplified;

You are the soul of that beauty!

Sunday, 30/06/2103, 12.23 p.m.

# THE IMPOSSIBLE.

Since unbridled joy and happiness
Are not how we achieve our perfection,
Pain has to be the mode of pathway
and feeling
By which we do reach greatness;

Thus pain is a finer, more prestigious quality
And experience
Than joy or happiness –
Pain hence becomes the ultimate emotion;

We can then, only define pain,
The ultimate emotion, as Love,
Love embodied deeply,
But as pain –
Seemingly inextricable within your core,
Resting deep inside you with resolve;

Yet those who assist others in pain,
with kindness –
To extricate its firmly-set lodging,
That state of Love called pain –
Go beyond Love itself:

What state do they hence reach,
Since it is humanly inconceivable to realize
 a state  greater than Love?

# **A POEM FOR A VERY SPECIAL PERSON**

You face,
And have faced hardship:

If we see challenges as important –
And they are –
Then the challenged person is very important:

Your challenges then,
Make you vital
And critical
To the world!

How important
And how serious
Will you be considered,
If you cope with your hardships?

So grave and imperative
Is your challenge
You become of infinite value
If you sincerely, honestly
Even intend to challenge your hardships!

## **A POEM FOR YOU.....**

You are sincere, kind and caring –
therefore, everything that belongs to me,
that is great –
my heart and its generosity,
and everything that belongs to the realm
and world of goodness belongs to you –
all of this is in your heart.

This is because your sincerity,
kindness and goodness
is a magnet of consideration that wins all
great phenomenon –
your heart has thus won all;
it has won Love:
Love is in your possession;

And since Love is *everything,*
and you have in your heart's possession the
magnet that attracts the great,
you can draw to yourself, to your heart,
everything worthwhile and meaningful
that can be desired in the universe!

What then, is the stature
Of someone
Sincere, kind and good?

This person has seen through the darkness
The world intended for him or her,
And due to their virtue,
The brightest of things,
Their universe is incandescent,
Brilliantly lit;

He or she is thus master of all that they witness
With their eyes, mind and heart,
And yet their hearts harbour even more,
An infinite quantity of salutary qualities,
That can be applied in myriad situations;

The question then arises,
Which cannot truly be answered;
What is the real capacity
Of the good, kind and loving person?

# A POEM FOR A CARE WORKER....

Thank you, for being so gentle,
Thank you for being so nice –
Meeting with you today for
Decades satisfaction will suffice:

Thank you, for your consideration,
Thank you for your kindness and care,
I will always, always appreciate you,
My heart to you is laid open and bare:

My dear helper, you are swell, and fine,
My dearest, you in caring are most wise;
The angels, witnessing you
Raise to heaven their joyous cries!

But most, most of all, I have to say
That you have time for the unwanted,
This makes you very, very special
And honoured, elevated and exalted!

Thursday, 14/11/ 2013, 2.10 p.m.

## A POEM FOR A GENEROUS WOMAN

## ON HER WEDDING DAY, with Love.

Your great heart I can see clearly,
it is in the world – out;
A great, great heart,
one that the world cannot do without;

Your kindness and love transforms
you into a human gem,
That illuminates me, your friends
and family – each of them;

Your smile is a beautiful quality
not to be faulted –
And a stream of praise is due to you,
not to be halted;

You seek only to give – not for profit,
but to benefit,
For the depressed a cure – majestic,
from where they sit;

Your goodness is your greatness – your tremendous wealth –
That brings most of all good cheer, good spirits and good health;

I know now – through you – what is wealth and what is poverty;
For care and consideration conferred is, real freedom and liberty;

I came upon you in my journey, if truth be measured, by chance –
That such goodness could come to me – by mere circumstance!

Your life is an authentic life with its authenticity intensified;
And your project is unity – to bring love and joy – as one, unified;

Let no cause, no event arise that takes away your qualities;
Be as you are – remain thus – sacrosanct should remain your abilities!

## **A POEM FOR AN ASPIRING STUDENT.**

You can only do your best
In any examination or test:

Whatever your intended profession or trade,
Your aspirations are already realized and made –

Already in the Unseen,
for you are a noble soul,
With your nobility making your
world whole;

And this right now, not in the future distant:
Hence you've achieved all ambition in an instant!

All this was achieved merely by your noble intention,
Which the Unseen accepts, without any contention:

Your nobility threw on the Universe flowers,
And it gave you everything, with all its Powers!

# A POEM FOR YOU..........

The sun has not come out today;
It is dark and cloudy and raining –
It is miserable weather,
Or so it seems:

I live in my heart and from and through my heart
And my heart has seen so much wrongdoing
It feels the world's pain – the result is that
Most intelligent observers would say that
My heart's season is winter:

However, when I see a rose,
or a picture of a tiger;
I am reminded of the Genius of the universe
That It can bring such beauty to being;
With this evident lovely and wonderful intention of this Genius;

Surely It meant well when the world was created
And fashioned and shaped by It;
Surely this Genius is good, kind and loving –
Greatly good, kind and loving;

And who knows that with Its tremendous goodness, kindness and Love,
This great Genius will not create another world;

After we have destroyed this one,
A wonderful and lovely new world,
Which It will give to those who proved themselves deserving in this world and life?

The reason I say this is because this creative Genius is out of the clamorous reach of mankind –
It is still alive, sacrosanct and whole, and cannot be defeated,
And can mobilize It's powerful and beautiful forces at anytime:

The very fact that It created this great world is evidence that this Genius cannot be defeated:
And the fact that this world was designed to persist in history;

Unsoiled and beautiful
Is proof that the goodness, kindness and
Love of this Genius
Was meant to exist forever;

And the shaper and fashioner
of the rose and tiger,
And the great beauty we see in the universe,
Surely this prodigious Genius has
had its conscience affected;

And with this conscience and responsibility
For Its entire work,
Will not let perpetrators of wrongdoing,
who have marred the face
of Its beautiful creation;

Go scot-free without giving account.
And for those who tried to maintain
It's intended beauty
Will it not create a handsome reward?

Will it not create another sacrosanct world,
Similar, identical to this one
In variety of flora and fauna?

So, despite my witnessing of
pain in the world,
It is sunshine and spring for my heart,
And I can live in my heart and from and
through my heart with peace of mind;

What I am saying is,
Whatever the inner and outer weather,
The good, kind and loving Genius
That brought the universe into being,
Represents, always, spring and sunshine for
mankind!

It is Beauty that is functioning,
And with a Promise —
All Beauty
Is a Promise!

# **A POEM FOR YOU...............**

Generosity is the basis
Of any giving –
It substantiates beauty,
And giving is the basis of healing.
Your tremendous beauty
Gives out very generously –

It gives out
Love,
Kindness
And goodness;

Therefore,
You heal
With your beauty;

How does one then
Define you?

As a flower,

Because
A flower
Heals
With the vast giving
And generosity
Of it tremendous beauty!

## **TO A GIRL ABOUT TO GRADUATE,**

## **FROM HER PARENTS........**

Your education is almost complete –
But, to us, you are complete anyway,
Today;

In fact, you were complete in everything
The day you were born, and we brought
you home from the hospital:

You were beautiful then,
And since you are
Becoming even more accomplished now,
You are growing even more beautiful!

Friday, 03/06/2011, 1.50 p.m

## MY ACHIEVING THE IMPOSSIBLE......

Today I achieved the impossible:
When something is immeasurably lovely,
Exceedingly enticing
And astoundingly beautiful;

The strongest bond is constructed with it
And it is very difficult
To part from it —
And to remain apart from it:

You, my dear,
Are immeasurably lovely,
Exceedingly enticing,
And astoundingly beautiful;

And I am drawn near you
By the strongest — the strongest —
of attractions,
And to break away from you
Is tremendously difficult:

Yet, I achieved the impossible today:
I left your side – yes, I left your side –
To come to work – and yes, successfully,
Remained apart from you for the best part
of a whole day;


I successfully paid attention to other things –
However that isn't my crowning,
The fact is that for a brief moment,
A very fleeting span of time;

I was oblivious of you,
An impossibility!
That is my glory!
That is my enactment of the truly
impossible!

Very, very impressive,
And very, very remarkable,
Are they not,
My great achievements today?

## **A POEM FOR A YOUNG PERSON LEAVING SCHOOL.**

You are making your own way in life,
Independent, beautiful and strong –
Just like the moon,
which is Independent,
beautiful and strong:

And yet,
the moon has a single function –
It can only appear in the night sky –
It is limited in scope –

You though,
Can appear beautifully, handsomely
In the peoples hearts,
Their minds,
Their souls
And their eyes
At any time!

## **A POEM FOR A HELPFUL PERSON.**

I am thinking of you —
Thinking of the good
Is in turn good for me —
My feelings incline towards loveliness;

And the good
Seriously try to overcome
Their trials and difficulties —
And that is inspiration for me:

You are thus
Goodness and inspiration
In my life!

You provide a vital link
Between my challenges
And my confrontation
And overcoming of them;

Goodness is the foundation
Of my movement towards success,
And inspiration the smoothly spent fuel
For my aspiring momentum!

Nothing valuable perishes:

Your heart is the lodging
Of your goodness,
A golden heart
Whose value will never diminish
In life or death!

Goodness is thus guarantee of immortality!

## **YOU, DESCRIBED........**

When I am near you,
You are like the moon –
Very, very beautiful:

When I am far away from you,
You are like a star –
Further away,
But still
Very, very beautiful!

## **JUSTICE AND YOU.**

It is right,
And righteous,
For mankind to greatly Love
Kindness,
Goodness
And loveliness:

It is right then that every man, woman
and child in the world
Should find it correct
With all their heart
To love you,
Who are kind, good and lovely:

The one who does not love you
Has made a great error in judgement
And ought to be pitied,
And forgiven,
For this person
Has not been just —
Has not done justice —
To their own humanity and personality.

## **A THOUGHT FOR YOU...**

In my heart,
My love for you
Has more expanse,
More volume
Than space;
Is more instructed
Than a great poet's verse;
Is more unrestrained
Than the free and powerful oceans –

Why do I love you?

Because you are a good person –

And this is how
All good people
Should be loved –
By everyone!

# A POEM FOR GOOD PEOPLE

## ... LIKE YOU....

The most precious attribute is goodness –

Goodness heals, like a flower –
Indeed, it is the blossoming of the personality.
Beauty is the best source of healing and medication –
Therefore your goodness makes you beautiful.

The human being, however, is greater than a flower –
Hence, if a flower is ultimate beauty,
How beautiful is the good human being?

Therefore there must be a heaven –
For, what other environment deserves you,
The good person?

Therefore there must be a hell –
For, what other land will deserve those unlike you?

But, there is no hell –

Because of humanity's goodness,
In which you play a key and critical role,
Because of our beauty,
All the badness in the world is overcome,
Supplanted, and reduced to nothing.

Our goodness has erased
Everything bad from the world,
So that only good remains,
And so hell is simply a purification by Love.

# **A POEM FOR A KIND PERSON.**

Today I met you,
And I could go no further:
I do not have to go further to achieve:

For, what life station, what experience
Can possibly lie beyond that of
Received kindness?

Not that of Love,
For kindness is Love –
Kindness incorporates Love;

Certainly not greatness,
For kindness is greatness realized;

Thus, I reached the limit
Of human experience
In meeting you today;

I have reached the end
point of life and living;

Your kindness has completely contoured
Hewn, shaped, fashioned
And coloured me;

And I can go no further –
I am the finished article –

I have therefore blossomed – into a permanent bloom –
Due to the kindness you showed me today –
It only requires this memory to keep this blossom thriving!

How extensive though will be my reach,
How far can I myself extend:

If I try to reciprocate your kindness?

## **A POEM FOR HEALING.**

When one is beset by sorrow and grief
To a most heightened degree,
And pain fully suffuses your being,
Where does the individual turn?

To the light of vast and brilliant Love,
Permanently lit
and its warmth and illumination
always available in the universe.

Sorrow and grief and pain
Are simply your trembling and exceedingly excited trepidation
In the anticipation of the loveliest drowning
in the ocean of Love.

Our hurt is also our unfamiliar separation
from this phenomenal world,
to which we are so habituated,
because we are to be introduced to the
unusual phenomenon of
Love.
We are introduced to another unfamiliar
world,
The world of Love.

And our difficulties and tribulation in life are our unfamiliarity
With this unorthodox world of Love.

And the world of Love is strange —
unorthodox — it has to be —
Because when all doors are shut to us,
The entrance to Love is wide open;

A contrasting fact after our habitual experience of impasse in life —
The fact and idea that the wonder of Love awaits us when we are beleaguered:

To have the knowledge that we possess the ocean of Love in our very midst, and with immediacy, when suffering Is the greatest exception possible in human existence.

And all good and great things are unconventional and exceptional.

And this world of Love,
That we are welcome to and abandon ourselves to in our pain,

Lies simply, within the tumultuous,
ubiquitous world of nature –
And nature surrounds us in every direction
we care to perceive.

Love created each blade of grass,
And Love is fully represented in
It's flushing greenery;

Love is wholly present in the
glowing solidity of a rock,
And it finds anchorage in
the firm mountains;

In the merest plant Love
reaches manifold completion,
The plant's great Love pouring
out of it in torrents;

Torrential too, is the outpouring of Love
From the eyes of that majestic wonder,
an animal;

And the human being is such a huge
repository of Love,
That even your enemies unconsciously exude
Love copiously in your direction:

Do they not yet contain within themselves
the experience of perfect Love,
gathered as an infant?

What then can we say about the
enormous content of Love
In a little child, the good adult,
the stars, the galaxies,
And the Creator of Love, God?

And all this Love – the entire range of this
fathomless Love –
Was expressly meant for you,
The person facing trial and difficulties.

Love, in other words, is that most precious
entity, Beauty:
And we know that Beauty is the most
attractive, the strongest and
most prodigious fact:

And all forms of healing can be
defined as beauty:

The Beauty of Love
Is the finest source of solace, comfort and
alleviation known to man.

This whole Love, this boundless Beauty
Is particularly present, with content
overwhelming;

When you are tried with an onerous
experience –
Turn to this ever-present Love,
Which will take in its every guise
the deepest impression of Beauty;

And is present in everything around you,
Particularly when in pain and grief and
sorrow –

This Beauty, or, Love awaits you
to receive it–
It longs, ardently, to beautifully serve you!

# A POEM FOR A THOUGHTFUL PERSON

Your vast character
Is but a minute
Facet of your personality;

A huge, enormous personality;

And your personality
Is a smaller fragment
Of your heart —

An immense, colossal heart;

If your character is the greatest fragrance,
And your personality the most considerable flower,

What is your heart?

# **A POEM FOR A FRIENDLY PERSON.**

You are as a lamp
In the darkness today:

Your kindness obliterates
The opacity
People find themselves in,
And it lights up their path
By inspiration –

Inspired by your kindness,
These people can reach
Great personal heights –
They can travel far –

Hence, your kindness
Is the finest energy
That propels
Men, women and children
Out of their usual sphere and orbit
To a transcended one!

If kindness can impel salutary achievement,
How prodigious and great is it to
Consistently be kind?

And what level of gain
And honour himself or herself
Is the kind person on?

## HOW YOU BECAME GREAT : A POEM IN PROSE FOR A GOOD AND CONSCIENTIOUS CARE WORKER.

In the world there are very many beautiful people, animals, plants and things: beautiful flowers, the moon, the stars, little children, good mothers and fathers: all these are immensely beautiful.

By your kind speech, good actions, and virtuous thought, you have added to this world of Beauty, and have enabled it, by your tremendous conduct to magnify and grow larger in Beauty.

You have, through your humane behaviour and Love made the great Beauty of flowers, the moon, the stars, little children and good mothers even more beautiful.

It is this good character of yours that has made you a great individual and person.

# **GOODNESS**

Why are the good men
And good women
Nowhere to be seen?

The good men
And good women
Are dead:

*'The good man*
*'is alive*
*'even when carried*
*'to the home of the dead'* – Imam Ali;

Hence,
The good men
And good women
We actually see
Walking in our midst
Are immortal.

Sunday, 24/08/2014, 10.31 p.m.

# **A POEM FOR A FEMALE FRIEND.**

A flower is delicately created,
With the greatest Love,
And the utmost beauty
Is incorporated into its creation:

You too, my dear,
With your utmost beauty
Must have been created
With the greatest Love–

At the very least then,
You are equal to a flower!

## **A POEM FOR A YOUNG ADULT CHILD, RAISED WELL, AND HER MOTHER, ON THE CHILD'S BIRTHDAY.**

One day yearly you celebrate with your child her birthday –
You brought her to life, and her life has this to you to say:

That she has succeeded against all odds, against the grain,
And does, despite life's constant difficulty her dignity maintain:

That she works very hard and has endeavoured to do her best –
Through dedication, she has reached life's very essence and zest:

That she has grown beautifully and into more beauty will grow,
And on the foundation of youth the seeds of happiness sow:

That the world stands to gain from her
maturity and studied trade,
Because skill and finesse are from
fruition and good education made:

Be proud of your wonderful daughter –
be of her success the gleaner
Nothing more precious that is acquired
by life – and also, cheaper:

There is nothing, nothing more precious
than a good and loving child
And I hope to her virtue, love, and
kindness you are most reconciled:

Happy birthday dear, you have with
Mum this great day to share,
A good child gives the parent the
clothes of dignity, pride and joy to wear!

# **A POEM FOR A GOOD WOMAN.**

To look at your lovely eyes
With the briefest
Of fleeting glances
Is to become filled
With the most majestic beauty;

To look intently into your eyes
For a brief moment –
How wonderful would that be?

The eyes are the window of the soul –
I would then have knowledge of your soul,
And know that it is heaven bound,
Destined to adorn heaven
As one of its greatest wonders:

If your eyes are the finest beauty
And your soul a great sign of heaven,
What then are you?

You are simply,
A kind woman!


Sunday, 13/07/2014, 5.18 p.m.

# A POEM FOR THAT EVER-SURPRISING PERSON.......

We are all born beautiful,
as little children,
But begin to lose our essential greatness
when we grow slightly older –
Then, we need to regain our beauty;

One of the ingredients for
this is patience;

You are proof of practiced,
realized patience,
For you have retained and also,
regained much of your original
beauty as an adult;

And your practice of patience and its
aspirations retains the original
philosophy of the beauty you
possessed as an infant;

It is to witness the resuming of beauty in every adult in all humanity, regardless of colour, creed or religion;

This imperative patience has another term: courage:

And you plan for humanity, in your patience, is the Divine Plan,
For is not God patient, and awaiting every adult to assume their
great child-like
beauty again?

Thus – indeed thus – you share a platform with God in strategy and planning for mankind;

And surely this majestic and great shared stature with God is your right –
For, are you not a good mother?

## A POEM FOR YOU, IN PAIN.

*'You, a human being, are greater than the sun or moon..' (Quran)*

If difficulty comes your way,
Remember the sun –

The sun burns in agony day and night –
But it gives light to the world –
We find our way in the light of the
sun's pain;

You in your pain and sorrow
Burn,
But are the unseen sun
Greater than the cosmic sun in the sky –

The light in you that is more luminescent
than the sun
Is your patience and steadfastness in your
predicament'

Together with your optimism –
These great qualities are a source of hope
For the people around you,

And they can find their way through the
labyrinths of life
More effectively armed with hope –

You therefore are the sun
That more than gives more light
to the world,
Than the planetary sun:

For you illuminate the inward of people:
You must illuminate the universe more
beautifully then,
And create far greater solutions to the
winter of the world –

You in your pain
Are the great sun
That is the issue of the finest spring
Everyday,
For the world of man.

And your personality and character
Can be, at your bidding,
A perennial spring.

Thursday, 09/08/2012, 6.50 p.m.

# **A POEM FOR A LITTLE GIRL CHILD....**

Dearest, you make me feel better
Because when I see you
Or hear about you,
I am reminded
That you are more
Beautiful than a flower,
And stronger than a mountain:

You are more beautiful
Than any flower
And stronger than any mountain
Because you are loving and kind:

Love and kindness
Are stronger than anything in the world,
And because you love and are kind,
You are truly beautiful and powerful.


Love and best wishes,

Shakil, Wednesday, 03/08/2011, 3.34 p.m

## A POEM FOR A LITTLE BOY.........

Of all the things to know in the world,
You know a lot – you know most
About Love and kindness,
And you show this Love and kindness
To your parents,
Your brothers and sisters,
And to your friends.

To know about Love and kindness,
And then actually show this Love and kindness –
Love and kindness in your thinking,
Love and kindness in what you say
And Love and kindness in what you do –
Your Love and kindness –
Makes you, my dear,
Strong,
Powerful
And very handsome.

But it also makes you a scholar,
Or a truly learned individual,
Because you actually practice
Your knowledge!

Love and best wishes,
Shakil, 03 / 08 / 2011, 3.45 p.m.

## **ART.**

Art
Is the process —
The meditation,
The thought,
The heart,
The creativity
Of the artist
En-route
To beginning,
Proceeding with,
And finishing
A work of Art:

Art is also
The process —
The meditation,
The thought,
The heart,
The creativity
Of the partaker
En-route
To understanding,
And experiencing
A work of Art.

# **A POEM FOR MY TEACHER JANE.**

Jane, you have helped me
And been kind to me –
I found my way
In my English literature
Most surely
Due to the light
You cast upon my pathway;

The moon guides those
Lost at night
With its wonderful illumination,
They find sure footsteps
On their pathway
Due to the moon's great generosity;

And all – all – of the moon,
Orb or crescent –
Participates in the luminous, generous guidance;

All of you, Jane – all of you –
Your personality, character and knowledge
Generously guided me at College,
Which makes you no less than the moon –

And no less in beauty!

## A POEM FOR MY FRIEND, NOW OVERSEAS..............

The moon grows from sickle to shield
And then regresses from orb to crescent;

You appeared in the daylight
And disappeared in the night-time –

Both the moon and you are
brilliantly beautiful
In your emergence and withdrawal –

However, the truly beautiful,
In hiding,
Grows even greater in beauty:

The moon, crescent or orb, certainly does.
The proof of this maturing in beauty
Is that I revere the moon even more
When it emerges fully from being partial –

And I grace its atrophy from shield to sickle
With the greatest appreciation –
Thus, I dearly love you to an even greater extent.

When you appear from your disappearance
at night-time –

And, you have been separated from me,
Overseas for the last few years –
Again the proof that you've grown more
beautiful than ever
Is that I possess a vast, immense love,
More powerful than ever, for you!

And as all beauty grows,
This, my love,
Will mature
With the passage of time!

## A POEM FOR LITTLE CHILDREN, A GOOD WOMAN OR A GOOD MAN.

The moment I understood you,
My heart raced ahead –
To its greatest goal,
Fully achieving its difficult quest:

My mind's ardent searching and wandering
For the satisfaction of my intellect
Fulfilled at last ;

And my soul found its rest and peace.

For, you taught me the lesson of faith –

Faith is to forgive,
To be honest,
To be compassionate,
To be kind, caring and loving –

And who-so-ever possesses these qualities
Has perfected their faith.

You mission in life is goodness,
And you are the missionary of care –

Is it possible
To be led
To a greater faith than this?

## A POEM FOR SOMEONE WHO WORKS FOR THE NATIONAL SOCIETY FOR THE PROTECTION OF CRUELTY TO CHILDREN.

We, people,
Are all mirrors
To one another –

I see in your face
The greatest beauty,
Majestic generosity
And immense love –

Why?

Because you are a mirror
To little children!


Love and best wishes,

Sunday, 23/01/2011, 10.47 a.m.

# THE HUMAN BEING................

A thinker once said,
'Men, women and children
'are trees,
'their roots are their heads,
'growing towards the heavens !'

Each smile,
Kind word,
Good thought,
Loving action;

Every possible show of virtue
Is a fruit of the tree of heaven –
Is thus a fact of heaven,
It is heavenly substance!

Human beings cannot but help
Being heavenly!

# THINKING CORRECTLY.

Thought of truly,
A gentle pat on the back,
Or a kind word
To someone beleaguered
Is more precious
Than all the gold and diamonds
In the world.

Thus, we can ask,
How precious is the good heart?
And how beautiful?

## **OPPORTUNITY................**

Mankind !
This life's greatest possibility
Is the many, many opportunities
We have
To be good, kind and loving :

And greatest punishment —
The greatest regret —
Of the inhabitants of hell
Will be
An afflicted conscience
Telling hell's inhabitants
That they forsook
The opportunity
To show Goodness, Kindness and Love.

## **A POEM FOR A SICK PERSONS.**

You see your pain and sorrow
As fathomless,
As a bottomless source
Of sorrow:
But, sorrow has its beauty –
It makes you weep tears worth pearls;
And every good thought whilst sorrowing is
invaluable –

Sorrow's every pulse then is precious,
And valuable:
This is its beauty!

Hence if the source of your pain, troubles
and sorrow Is endless, infinite in scope,
And sorrow and tribulation can
be defined as beautiful,
You possess in the unending channel
of your trial
A prodigious amount of beauty –

And, sorrow being the most important experience
for men  women and children,
You have in your possession in your limitless
sorrow-
An immense quantity of beauty!

Thursday 10/07/2014, 6.03 p.m.

## A POEM FOR AN OLDER POOR ORPHAN, A VERY SPECIAL ANGEL……………….

Your existence has been full of strife,
And yet, you try to find your way in life –

You had to search, search, and
you saw every human quality,
And angels are kind – like and
with them you feel great humanity –

Unsupported, not helped,
you had to find your way,
That a little angel may have
in life an eloquent say –

This is courage, tremendous courage indeed,
That you planted for your future a brave seed –

She, or he who despite a hard life,
tries to recover,
Will, I hope, happiness and greatness discover;

If you require assistance,
please come to me –
I want you to be of every need
and trouble free –

I know that you will finish in life
or school your education,
Because hard work has fine
success as its translation –

I am here for you, always, as your friend –
And in friendship we'll be until the final end;

When you need a pillar to lean on,
I will be there:
Though weak, I am strong when
I have your beauty to bear;

My young friend, I wish you well,
please take care –
You've shown courage –
thus, you are the fairest of the fair!

## A POEM FOR SOMEONE WHO CAN JUDGE LOVE.

Today you feel pulverized – demolished, utterly brought down: in this situation then, you are fully deserving of Love:

Those who completely deserve Love, are they not the most fortunate of the fortunate?

Hence, your sorrow and grief is not an obstacle, but an open gate to experiencing the greatest phenomenon a human being can experience;

That is, in this state of sorrow and grief, you can fully feel and appreciate affection, consideration;

Goodness, Kindness and Love:

And your pain qualifies you to give judgment and weight to this greatest of experiences of loveliness;

Something otherwise beyond the abilities of men, women and children – are you not then made empowered in your tribulation?

And thus, the virtues you show, because of, and in-spite of your trial become suffused with golden qualities;

They become jewel-like: the most majestic and magnificent values can be put upon them:

How much do you actually achieve, and how much can you actually achieve when you experience the troubles of your life?

Thursday, 03/07/2014 7.57 p.m.

# **A POEM FOR THE GOOD WOMAN.**

Love is the most majestic and magnificent
Quality ever devised
In the history of the universe –

Love, in whatever quantity,
Is most beautiful,
Very easily surpassing
All other beauty in the cosmos:

How beautiful then,
Your personality,
Which is applied Love,
Love in action?

# A POEM TO THE WIFE I WILL NEVER HAVE................

I am faithful to you in Love –
The waves of the ocean
Learnt their fidelity to the shore
From the ardour of my loyalty;

The moon learnt from me its work –
The necessity to be incandescent,
A lamp in darkness,
For I only desire to hold you
When you are forlorn and crestfallen;

The sun learns from me,
And my vocation
Resignation at dusk,
Leaving the earth alone
After a glorious day
And then availing of opportunity at dawn –
For I resign
And opportunely
Leave you alone
In your beauty;
I only want to rise
To assist you
When you attempt to raise

Your stature in your world;

I am distant from you,
Yet of use —
I want to enable,
And en-skill you,
To be able to navigate the torturous, storm-ridden seas of the world;

Thus I am like the stars:
They learnt their navigational task
from my intention to attempt to ably
navigate life;

My real place is away from you,
Detached,
Yet present
In your midst when occasion demands —

Else,
We have no relationship
In my eyes.


Saturday, 19/10/2013, 10.45 p.m.

# **A POEM FOR ALL PATIENTS:**

## For people who have experienced health problems.

Only the most beautiful and most important
Thing, idea and fact
Can itself give rise to another beauty of magnitude –
And Love is the most beautiful and important
Thing, idea and fact of all;

Love then, it must be admitted,
Gives rise to, and is the cause of the gravest beauty;

At the birth of a little child, or star –
Both magnificently beautiful,
There is pain –
Who cannot say that this pain is caused by Love,
For only Love

Could give rise to such great beauty
Such as a little child or a star?

Your tremendous pain,
and the resulting illness
Thus have been caused by the greatest Love—
Thus, your pain and illness
Are the most beautiful events in the universe.

Your constant pain and the attendant illness
Mean that you are in a constant state of beauty and Love –
Therefore, Love and beauty being the most excellent and splendid
And critical of things, ideas and facts;

You have reached,
In your pain and illness,
Which arrived through Love,
The finest and greatest state
A human being can possibly achieve!

## **A GREAT UNION..........**

My eyes saw very well
Your comeliness;

My mind sensed very well
Your loveliness and intelligent words:

But, it was my heart
That truly understood,
And then admired
Your beauty;

And I had to amplify my heart,
Purify it,
To truly understand your beauty,
For only purity
Can recognize purity
And only greatness
Can recognize greatness:

To be one with you
Is a physical,
Intellectual and emotional experience,

But, most of all,
And including the dimension
of the physical,
Union with you is a spiritual
phenomenon.

And a spiritual being has yearnings –
For greater elevation:
In other words it desires to
serve humanity,
And be close to God.

How much would the unification
Of two sincere spiritual beings
yearn for?

Particularly, since their togetherness
Strengthens and empowers them?

How much will they eventually achieve
as a unit?

# A POEM FOR WOMANITY.....

To me,
You are immense and vast in personality:

Of great expanse in character –
For, you are a woman.
But your greatness is Truth,
And your greatness will only emerge when
you embrace the Truth,
Which is kindness.

And when you do embrace kindness,
Your personality and character
Externalize and internalize their true nature–
As huge and giant-like –
For, is not the Truth strong and powerful?

Thus, your kindness is strong
and powerful,
And naturally shapes and contours your
personality and character:

To show huge strength and vast power-
That is in keeping
With your nature,
That of being a woman!

Thus the terms 'woman'
'A woman's personality' and
'A woman's character'

All have a dual definition –
Strength and power,
Which taken together,
Amount to her beauty!

# A POEM FOR YOU, A GOOD WOMAN.

Because you are a woman,
It is correct and right that the finest
music, poetry and Art
Is devoted to you:

For, a woman powerfully embodies in
her womanliness
The most learned amalgam of Love,
humanity, beauty and intelligence –
Some, on whom good fortune shines,
become mothers;

Then, as mothers, their consideration,
their loving is perfect.

Hold this phenomenon, woman, close to
your eyes and close to your heart,
And wonder at her incredible creation
and composition –

The woman is a phenomenon of the greatest riches, personality, and the most precious words and actions.

And when she allows a man close to her, and into her world,
He ought to stand joyful and grateful:
For that feeling of closeness to her is a wonder in itself:

To hold hands with her,
Meet her gaze
Are majestic,
magnificent experiences indeed.

A woman was made for just one –
only one – consideration:
Love: nothing less;

She is the great master of humanity, worthy of the most intense, intelligent and wise study;

Only one being can contend with the
good woman for earthly sovereignty:

A little child.
And her final and appropriate
allowance,
Through all phases of her life,
Is great dignity, her natural right.

The adult woman, this being of
utmost potential,
Should be allowed
Every facility and assistance
by mankind
To rise to her birthright:

Greatness,
And must be allowed every able help
To immerse herself in her beauty,
And then, fully dignified,
Express her beauty.

## **A POEM FOR YOU IN YOUR SORROW.**

Sorrow
Is the most beautiful emotion,
For, it causes flowers to grow.

And, flowers do naught
But show Love:

What could be a greater accomplishment
Than sorrow then?

And, a great accomplishment
Such as Love –
The greatest attainment –
Can only emerge
From something equally great –

Thus, your sorrow
Is equal to Love –
That is why it is the most important
Of human events, experiences and
occurrences!


Sunday, 15/09/2013, 10.01 p.m.

## A POEM FOR YOU, A KIND WOMAN – A TREMENDOUS HUMAN BEING.

Take my poetry to your heart –
It will find a natural terrain, resting place
and home there;

My poetry is of Love, and your heart loving–
Your heart will give my poetry polish
and brilliance,
For that is what a loving heart does
to anything it touches:

But the poetry of Love – my poetry;
Is already luminescent –
Anything done with even a hint of Love
always is;
So how do you impart to my poetry
A greater shine and brightness?

A loving heart is vast enough to contain the
heavens and the earth-
In a loving heart hence live millions of
wonderful angels –
So your loving heart opens up my poetry to
an angelic audience,

An audience interminable in number and immortal:

My poetry thus is made eternal and immortalized by its reception in your loving heart:

With a loving heart, you are a true reader, receiver of Poetry –

In other words, the millions of beautiful angels in your loving heart mean that you are deserving of the stature of bearer of angels –

You, with a loving heart, bring angels to this world!

Friday, 15/11/2013, 12.23 p.m.
YMm

## A POEM FROM A DOG TO ITS OWNER..........

Hi ! its me, why!
Dogs do not write poems,
But I can always try!

Dogs do not speak,
But your heart's attention
In this poem I seek:

I cannot – ever – talk,
But always to you, my friend,
I will run and walk –

I may be without speech,
But you've cared for me so much,
Care to other dogs I can teach –

Your care for me
I understand so well,
I now roam freely!

And I know that you love me:
If I could speak,
I would call you Mummy! (Or Daddy).

## A POEM IN PROSE FOR MY FEMALE FRIENDS.

You are many, many, good things: but, most of all, you are kind. Of all the great gestures a human being can make, kindness is the greatest and finest.

And you are repeatedly kind; your constant kindness creates beauty, and a creator can only create what is substantially already within herself or himself:

Thus, you are beautiful yourself.

Of all beautifying measures, kindness is the best. And you are very, very powerful:

An act of kindness beautifies not only the individual you are being kind to, but the entire universe as well.

This indicates the vast power and strength of a thought, word or act of kindness.

Now, your ability to be kind is infinite: you only need the opportunity to behave thus; hence your capacity to become beautiful is also infinite.

If through your acts of kindness you are most majestic, and you possess a limitless potential to do so, and be so, how incalculably beautiful are you?

# A POEM OF THANKS FOR A KIND CAFE ASSISTANT..................

I arrived at the cafe today –
Despondent;

But, sometimes, we encounter, unexpectedly,
A great spiritual sustenance:

I saw your lovely face,
And your beautiful eyes introduced me
To your soul and heart –
Particularly, a heart of gold, precious
Because of the Love in it –

And your smile gave me this Love;

Your smile was an arrow tip –
Its Love pierced my own heart,
And all my despondency
Poured out of me,
Away from me;

You freed me with your smile,
With your heart of Love.

Then, your ample, vast heart
Arrested me,
Confined me
Within its domain
And committed havoc upon me –
It assaulted me with the greatest Love,
Gave me no respite from its great beauty,
And left me nothing except
Beauty and Love;

How?

You smiled at me again!

Thursday, 22/09/2011, 1.46 p.m.

# **A POEM ON LOVE........**

I thought Love would set me free –
And free to revel in life:

Alas, Love was jealous
And wanted me all to itself;
I could not concentrate on anything
except Love –
I could not even concentrate on myself,
I had to be consumed by Love:

I could not work towards any goals,
Think anything,
Or say anything
Or be anything;

Love wanted, all to Itself,
My powers, abilities, speech and actions;

I could not even breathe for myself –
Myself I had to leave far, far behind:

And so I died, dying in Love:
And so I had to live,
As a dead person:

And now my powers, speech,
actions and abilities
Are those of a deceased person;

How can a dead man be creative,
speak, act and show intellect?

Is that not remarkable?
And yet, I do so —
I thus show salutary qualities:
I am replete with ongoing achievement!

Love therefore made me an
amazing human being,
More amazing than I would have been
without Love:

I owe Love my death,
But to Love I also owe
A real, authentic life;

That incredibly has its foundation
In the Greatest, Most Merciful Unseen:
The greatest miracle of all.

Look at my life: look at the results of experiencing Love!

And this greatness, Love, can only issue
From such an unimaginably incredible locus and origin;

As the Magnificent Unseen!
Love deserves to!

## **A POEM WRITTEN FOR YOU, UPON WITNESSING AN INFANT WITH ITS GOOD MOTHER.**

Do you think that Love desired that you be ineffective, unsuccessful, feeble?

Love you were born powerfully empowered with, replete;

Love is always resident in your heart;
your Love you can manifest at any time;
To Love is to be effective,
to Love is to be eminently successful,
to Love is to be strong beyond strength;

Love called you and Love is your calling –
Think, see, feel and speak
with Love in your mind and heart–
then nothing will escape you,
and you have embraced everything;

Love is your most ample crown,
it is your sufficient treasury –
a treasure that is endless, infinite –
Love is the Holy Grail that everybody
can find and arm themselves with;

There is no better weaponry for capturing kingdom, nations, the earth, the universe with –

But most of all, you conquer the domain of greatest magnitude with Love –
the human heart:

Love is your real, authentic nature;
It is the cornerstone of your natural personality and character;

This Love must be manifested if you are to realize yourself.

Love automatically severs you from the untoward, and brings you, in this earthly existence, to radiant celestial living –

Love naturally embodies within itself kindness and goodness, and thus it is instantly sane, the acme of sanity;

It makes you the healer of mankind and animals: medicinal: providing the perennial need of the universe and all in it.

Whatever you study, whatever your vocation, what-so-ever your lifestyle;

Love is what you aim at, and undertake to manifest, consciously or unconsciously —

For, it is the most magnificent and greatest of human callings — and all human beings are called to magnificence and greatness.

Love makes all beings divine,
truly spiritual, truly artistic —
For, each moment of Love speaks
eloquently of the nature of the Godly:

And one ascends to the very summit of achievement, and each thought, action or word becomes endlessly fertile, expanding and growing infinitely ;

Each moment with Love is a victory, the Loving person victorious over every Impediment —

Love brought the universe into being, and in Love will it end:
And if, you Love, you are in tune with the original moment of creation and beyond the eternal: eternity: then, you truly ranscend.

Love is the most basic building block of personal greatness and significance, and it is that composition's most advanced stage.

Thus you are in the process of creating the most beautiful structure, and in possession of the finest complete edifice — both at the same time:

You are a consummate architect in Love — yet more, in any endeavour!

Love is loftiest thought of the great ones —
the little children, good mothers and fathers,
the saintly, the Prophets and God:

It is these great ones most lofty aim to think,
speak and act on Love —
And Love is easy, for anyone, to aim at —
it only needs us to institute willpower;

and contact the Divine in our hearts, and
then we are league and concert with the
finest and most magnificent:

Love then, is the greatest beginning, the
greatest ongoing viability, and the greatest
end or terminal for all that is human,
animal, plant, angelic and the planets!

Wednesday, 30/10/2013, 9.14 p.m.
yMm

## **A PROSE POEM FOR THE DISABLED....**

Quite, quite, disabled? Well everything created in creation was fashioned with Love in mind!

This entire amount of Love and its powerful original source was made just for you, just for you, the disabled person in mind.

Accept your disability in the light of the huge amount of Love in the universe and world:

The Love of little children, animals, plants, the moon, the stars, rocks, the pavements – all which emanate an endless, copious stream of Love;

Bear in mind the inestimable Love of good parents, kindred spirits, and if you like, the continuous flow of Love from God.

Feeling this generosity of the universe deep inside you, and awash with this great and immense Love, you will dispense with your pre-occupation with the severe affliction of disability and instead begin to focus exclusively upon the beautiful:

You will start to wonder about the wondrous: the beauty of Love. This concentration is all-healing in itself.

And this great Love present in the universe was especially created for you, because, being disabled, you are the perfect recipient of beautiful Love.

Try and access, and feel this immense Love, which truly exists, and feel it in your heart and mind, pouring in torrents towards you.

This great Love is ultimate beauty – there is no more majestic a beauty – and thus it is ultimate solace and healing for the pain of disability;

It fully incorporates kindness, goodness and consideration – especially for you, now disabled.

Knowing that the most magnificent thing in the universe, human or Divine – Love and its beauty – belongs solely to you will give you the drive, courage and valour to cope with your disability.

It will maintain your dignity, and because you are the sole, single reason for this Love, you become a truly honoured individual.

Everything, every single entity in the universe was created for you, with Love:

There are many Truths, but one of the most important Truths is that Love can defeat the most unlikely odds:

Love can successfully take on all odds!

Thursday, 17/07/2014, 12.34 p.m

# A THOUGHT FOR VALENTINE'S DAY

Your face has the loveliness of a flower
The luminescence of the moon in the dark Sky
And the radiance of the sun at noon –
Your face clearly shows tremendous beauty–
(And you smile!)

However, your heart has greater qualities than your face –
Your heart is courageous,
kind and considerate,
And filled with Love –

In your beauty,
You are a practical symbol
Of the most precious qualities human beings can employ or embody;
You are a living symbol
Of what it is to be an anchor for humanity –

Thus, whichever way anybody sees you
and experiences you,
They have to see you as wholly
beautiful —
And every day of the year you retain
and show your great beauty —


On any day, hence,
on any day of the year
Whenever any man witnesses you,
Or speaks to you,
You are his Valentine:

Happy Valentine's Day!

## A TREE PLANTED ON THE EUROPEAN MAINLAND IN 1900.
## A POEM IN PROSE :

You may wonder, how could I grow so tall and verdant on a bed of dirt and a diet of air washed down with plain ordinary rain?

You may wonder what beautiful inner world impels me to usher blossoms every year, without fail;

You may wonder what great ambition and hope gives me the drive – gives me the impetus – to adorn the world and bedeck it with blossoms, unfailingly, inevitably, for the past hundred and fourteen years?

People looking on must think that I am satisfied, happy and at peace, and oblivious; but no, I am filled with sadness:

I have seen men do terrible things to one another, particularly in my early to late teens and in my early middle age.

Moreover, they say that youth is impressionable and that what has been impressed upon it has repercussions, ramifications, and if harmful, is inerasable;

A disturbed youth has deleterious effects that last a lifetime; and any later pain is merely, simply, a compounding experience;

And so, I have been driven mad by what I have witnessed before I came of age:

Therefore, it is not satiety and success and optimism that impels me and gives me momentum and dynamism, but my accomplished madness!

Wednesday, 02/02/2011, 11.08 p.m.

# A VALENTINE'S THOUGHT FOR YOU

This Valentine's Day,
A very special angel in heaven
Will have very special thoughts for you;

He will fall in love with you,
Totally and absolutely,
Will cherish you,
And place you in choicest domain in the universe —
His heart —
An angel's heart;

However, I hope, that on earth
This Valentine's Day,
There is one man who resembles that angel above
Nay, who even supersedes that angel —
Human beings at their greatest are greater than angels —

A great man who fully understands you
as his cherished dream completely
realized,
And in gratefulness for his elevation
and majestic honour
Raises your heart within his heart
To the highest station he can;

He will give you his unqualified love,
And with the noblest,
purest strength and power:

Esteems you and gives you the rank
Of his beloved.




With love and best wishes.

## A WEDDING DAY THOUGHT FOR YOU........

Are you today a flower,
Or a sunset?
No. You are a power,
Beauty we've again met;

Are you the moon,
Or a lioness?
No. You're the musical tune
That is largesse;

What are you then?
Are you what we see?
Yes. You're to women and men
A comfort, consolatory;

Therefore you're a soul,
A woman with heart,
Great and whole,
A woman beautifully apart!

# A WEDDING WISH FOR A LADY....

'Just as darkness inspires the moon and stars, I hope that difficulty inspires your brilliance;

Just as flowers by nature exhale fragrance, I hope that you naturally emanate Love;

Just as the sun consumes itself to bring light and warmth, I hope that your dutiful life is consumed in bringing hope and solace;

Just as a river cannot prevent itself reaching the sea, I hope that you progress inevitably to the ocean of success;

Just as the clouds absorb moisture and then precipitate, I hope that you sup the best knowledge and then shower and bestow it upon the world;

Just as the dignified sky covers every horizon, I hope that infallible Truth canopies your whole universe;

Just as the unshakable mountains tower over the plains, I hope that your tremendous good character is towering in our difficult age;

Just as plants work hard to grow, flower and fruit, I hope that your conscientious industry leads to majestic achievement;

Just as little children are very great, I hope that in your beautiful nature there remains something of the child;

Just as being kind is being genuinely spiritual, I hope that your virtuous character is innately suffused with kindness;

Just as those who practice implacably become skilled, I hope that your hard-won willpower becomes your skill;

Just as the great ones have only heart, I hope that your ample heart realizes the greatness awaiting it;

Just as the healing rose has thorns, I hope that your considerable, comforting beauty is protected;

And just as in Truth God is Merciful and Loving, I hope that you are always in His Merciful and Loving gaze!'

# **A WISH.**

## A poem for friends.

I will relax,
In and out of your presence,
But, I will be aware –
I will not stop
Visualizing –
And feeling;

Then, I can appreciate you,
Your significance,
And precious existence.

## A WOMAN OF PROMISE AND POTENTIAL..............

If one needs to fall in love,
It ought to be with a woman to whom
Love means everything, and is,
moreover, a person with promise and
potential;

For then, her sense of responsibility and
need to prove herself is uppermost, and
at the very least, she benefits;

And in train with her need to realize her
ambitions and aspirations, she confers
equal Love in all directions, including
that due her partner:

I have lived in London for over forty
years,

Taking into my heart and soul the hearts and souls of its gracious inhabitants, of every hue, creed and culture;

My Love voluntarily poured out for them, for humanity all;

After loving the people of London, I loved their cultures, creeds and manners:

And a moment arrived in 1991, When the infinite store of Love I promised humanity arrived at a crescendo and overflowing point:

When I met her, the scholar at the University of London;

She introduced, fully – her kindly mind, heart and soul – to me, in her first glance at me – when she smiled, with her developed  generous instinct;

With that extreme largesse and generosity of that smile, I knew her – completely;

I knew her, her promise and her potential –
I recognized her significant nature immediately:

Her grace and kindness issued copiously, as she spoke to me;

Her passion for imparting Love to an individual, stranger or not, Love to all, strangers or not, I understood from that initial beautiful smile, and her intentions she proved to me, when speaking to me;

She was accomplished – in her reading of Art, literature and science and contoured her learning with her humanity;

She was replete in her exchanges and interactions with men and women, all whether untoward or good, she wished well, forgave and loved –

Her promise and potential, at its base was founded upon Love, and at its apex would be solely devoted to Love;

The University of London was the conduit or channel to impart this Love –

Every single instance of my reciprocation of her grace was met with utmost gratitude and humility, so much did she know that Love was special:

I, the confirmed purveyor of Love – a most faithful and streaming Love; had met his match:

We held hands, and I looked into her eyes;

Holding hands with her overlapped the immensity of two feeling minds, hearts and souls, into one irrevocable unity and looking into her eyes gave me a clear window into the greatness of womanhood;

She brought to me wonderful tidings of a pure, pristine Unseen, and imprinted on my heart and mind the beauty of that Unseen;

Sorrow, at this stage I did not know if she had experienced much of – but surely it is in sorrow that such a kind nature would have matured.

And she was just twenty-two, on the threshold of life, on the cusp of the fulfilment of promise, potential and intellect;

And I loved her for her promise and potential, as much for what she had done for me within just two hours of our meeting—

And I Love her to this day, as much as I came to Love her in those first two hours:

It is not possible to exceed infinity —
In my case, an infinite Love I had arrived at, so quickly!

# **ADVICE TO A YOUNG FRIEND.**

It is sometimes normal, expected, to be of bad character:
It is thus unusual, and extraordinary, to be of good character!

And good character is not located in the brain,
Nor is it a facet of intelligence –
Its locus is deep, deep within the heart:

And the greatest surprise is that the heart can be broken,
Yet become whole again, stronger,
And give out yet more kindness and Love than ever before.

You are more significant than ever before when you display goodness after trial and tribulation –
This is the best way and manner of surpassing yourself,
And performing the impossible:

The broken heart then, is not the path to sadness, but happiness —
For he or she who rises above their difficulties;

And yet expresses good character
Realizes the tremendous secret of human existence —
They realize and practice the great purpose for which human beings were created:

Therefore do not treat sadness and problems as losses,
But as opportunities for your life to become most significant,
without parallel;

The key then, to human greatness is willpower,
Together with the practice of good Character:

Goodness, Kindness and Love.

# **YOU...**

The moon and stars
Never say
'Why do we necessarily
'have to always illuminate
'the heavens,
'and always sparkle,
'gem-like?'

The moon and stars
Just *are* magnificent;

And you never say
'Why do I necessarily
'always,
'have to possess
'the quality of appearing,
'and being beautiful?'

You just *are* magnificent
In your beauty!

## AN ANALYSIS OF THE BEAUTY OF A GOOD WOMAN.

To attempt to perfectly understand you,
I defer analysis of your looks and beautiful nature:

True beauty is really extant, grows, and remains forever –
I can only appreciate and revel in the truth in your beauty:

It has to be taken in entirely, in one glance,
And one prolonged, sustained meditation –
Beauty least requires analysis – it is way beyond that particular need to be visualized with clarity;

An approach that works most well is to say that it needs appreciation, thoughtfulness and utmost consideration —

To give respect is to foster almost total understanding:

I do not consider analysing your goodness and kindness.

Goodness and kindness are the soul, the central powerhouse of beauty, and to be understood —

And these are to be utterly respected, and thoughtfully adorned with honour;

These qualities cannot be analysed because they are an amalgamated power;

Above all powers, and power which is beautiful is to be administered and applied, not analysed;

And then, above all, esteemed and considered hallowed;

I refuse to — I do not want to — analyse any aspect of your splendid personality, Because, in your beauty, goodness and kindness you are free;

And those like you, who have found their freedom, should be allowed to roam and drift, with pleasure, in the very heavenly realm of this majestic freedom;

No, you do not need to be analysed, because analysis is not necessary in regarding you — that is to treat you with competent superficiality;

That is, it is to constrain, in my heart,
your beautiful freedom –
You are to be freed in your freedoms:

You only need is to be loved, a love that
comes to me with the greatest ease
and voluntarily, powerfully, and in
streams and copiously.

But the finest and greatest reason your
beauty is beyond the need for analysis,
is that it is true authentic beauty –
Like that of a little child, a flower or the
Love of a good parent;

This beauty needs only to be
appreciated, not analysed,
For only in that manner of
appreciation;

It remains whole, untarnished, its great
and wonderful mystery yet complete –
and sacrosanct,

That we can go on fully appreciating it,
and read its eloquence –
And riches – and then, always wonder
at its wondrous nature!

Can beauty *ever* be analysed?
It is like analysing the Truth,
For 'beauty is Truth,
'and Truth is beauty!' –

Beauty can but be cherished!
The desire to cherish
Makes the cherished one more
intelligible!




Monday, 10/09/2012, 2.17 p.m.

# **AN ESSENTIAL RESOURCE OF LOVE.**

The universe was created with Love.

A single electron – yes, a single electron –
Is so remarkable,
It could only have been created with Love:

If a single electron is so remarkable,
Look at the beautiful world that abounds around you;
Look at the stars, the moon, the sun, the plants, people, trees the sky, the trees, grass and the pavements –
All beautifully composed of these remarkable electrons;

How much Love then, surrounds you?

Even if an individual is against you,
He or she is composed of electrons,
And hence they are full of Love, and emit Love.

How much Love then, is in your proximity?

Thus, when forlorn, sad, or depressed,

Access the great resource and powerhouse of Love around you —
You will not fail in being placated.

A single electron is so wonderfully created,
It contains an infinite amount of Love —
The Love in a single electron is sufficient to placate and console you —
Then, look again at the remarkable, beautiful universe around you:

And everyone's personal world is vast and without end:

Hence, how great is the volume of Love in your world —
Your personal world,
To cajole, calm, and comfort you
In your hour of need?

Thursday, 07/11/2013, 1.03 p.m.

## AN ODE TO A MYSTIC.

Your words are the music of the heart,
set to the rhythm and melody
Of the fragrant forgiveness
That issues from you;

Your sighs are the longings of someone
beautiful,
Who has not divulged actually enough Love,
A great volume of Love
she actually possesses—
Enough to satisfy the needs of mankind;

Your stride is that of someone
with a huge goal,
A firm, pronounced step in the direction
Of the discovery of solace and comfort for
humanity;

Your weeping is that of someone who has
tasted
The bitter wine of difficulty and troubles,
And in her drunkenness ardently desires
To lighten the burdens of humanity
By carrying them on her own shoulders;

Your living is animated Beauty,
A fund so deep, so proffering,
It paves the way to gracious entry;

For every little child born,
and a peaceful and dignified exit
For every person that leaves
the earthly realm;

Your learning is that of the equable,
proportionate intellect,
That arbitrates and balances
With the sharp and accurate
diplomacy of goodness
Every predicament that besets mankind:

Your intellect is that of an able poet,
consummate scientist and dedicated mystic;
and your intellect is your heart;

Your intentions are simple and
simplified further, in action —
They are to witness even an
incremental proportion of Love
Added onto the world, and held onto, fast:

Thus, your humility is in your intentions;

Your vision is a hymn to little children,
A vision of authentic, true,
free and great individuals
Fully partaking of the earth,
and multiplying
The freedom, equality and opportunities
on earth for all;

Your attitude is rebellious, revolutionary,
That with the powerful weapons of
goodness, kindness and Love
Assails the fortresses of tyrants,
And one that gives liberty and guidance
To the common man and reduces despots;

Your politics is the fortification
of the immense goodness
In humanity and the realization
of its vast potential;
It is the kind goal of amity made
practical and widespread;

Your faith is in that heroic, great and universal: Love:

That heavily armed by Love and marching resolutely onwards,
And that canopied by the rain of Mercy,
Your faith is in Love: that strong, whole poetry for all seasons and things:

Love: that gently fierce, incessant and lithe:
Love: that of a Sun which with its brilliant radiance Issues a beautiful place on earth and eternity for all!

Wednesday, 26/03/2014, 1.43 p.m.

# AND A POEM FOR YOU..........

*'The sun and moon have been made subservient to you...'* ( Quran )

Men and women and children
Were created greater than the sun or moon
–
They can thus emulate these cosmic bodies,
Nay, surpass them in their conduct!

When the moon
Falls in the morning,
Its friend the sun
Picks up the responsibility of
Giving the world light;

In a friendship of two friends,
When one falls,
The other picks him up –
She shows responsibility;

The picking up itself
Is not physical,
But is made of understanding –
Understanding the person fallen;

I fell with you the other day,
And if you are my friend,
You will use your understanding of me
And pick me up —

Then, you will be like
The sun in the morning,
Or the moon at night,
Picking up the responsibility
Of the sun to light the world —
Or the moon to illuminate the dark —

If you show me
The light of understanding now,
You will be like the sun and moon —
beautiful!

Real, true beauty, in relationship,
Arrived at,
Is inerasable:
True friendship isn't made in a day,
And does not end in a day.

# FOR TEACHERS :
# A TEACHER'S GREAT STRENGTH......

One of the greatest human qualities
is a charitable nature,
And being great,
it is a portrayal of prodigious inner strength—

If ever lost for strength,
Draw on the resource
Of your tremendous strength —

A good deed
Is charity;

The natural world has vast power,
Seemingly greater than that embodied
By human beings —
However, according to the wise,
The doer of charity
Is the strongest person —
Stronger than rock,
And stronger than iron,
Which breaks rock,
Stronger than fire,
Which melts iron,
Stronger than water,

Which puts out fire,
And stronger than wind –
Which agitates water:

Your support
For your students
Is the finest good deed –
It is sublime charity,
And hence,
You are supremely strong!

If in your protégés hearts,
You have proved great strength,
How strong are you in your own heart?

You have proved your strength, a powerhouse,
And may draw upon it for greater happiness,
And succour in troubled times!

# **MY TEACHER'S SEASONS...............**

It is winter now,
And a greater season,
Spring, is approaching —

You are fabulous in your winter —
And even greater in your spring ;

That is,
You are fabulous when you are down,
And knocked out —
Yes, fabulous in your winter;

But you are even greater
When you recover from the blows of life —
That is, when you are in your spring ;

And then, one day,
The winters will lessen in intensity,
And hopefully become fragmentary,
And your seasons will largely be spring;

But guess what?

Your summer will arrive too,
And you will become even more majestic,
And even greater!

And your spring and summer will always permeate,

Your autumns and winters!

## **THE PURPOSE OF EDUCATION.**

Love was fashioned to unveil the Great Design —
Nay — divulge it —

He or she who is a true lover
Is close to the origin and nature of everything —
Close to the secret behind creation:

Now, being a true lover
Is given to many —
All little children, angels,
And those who re-gather the child-like state when adults;

So, the purpose of human existence
Can be outlined with certitude —
Whatever the endeavour,
Whether it be science, Art or spirituality,
The point is to remain a little child,
Or to re-gather this state as an older person.

Now, a little child knows most
about one knowledge:
Love;

Hence the purpose of human existence
Is to become a lover of God, man and nature:

To become a thoroughly good person.

Thus, any education,
Be it science, Art or spirituality
That does not take the one who practices it
To Love, goodness and kindness
Is on the wrong track and trajectory:

The one on the trail of Love
Has the universe,
God and nature serve him or her:
He or she is monarch over everything:

The purpose of education then,
Is to master everything
Through the practice of Love,
The finest erudition and learning,
Just as a little child in his or her knowledge of Love
Is master of everything!

YMm

## __BECAUSE: A POEM IN PROSE FOR GOOD PEOPLE.__

Because you always try to be kind, the gates of everlasting mercy have opened wide to you;

Because of your tremendous good nature, Love has found its natural resting place – inside your beautiful heart;

Because you listen with good intentions, to others, honour has decided to wholly belong to you;

Because you are of a sweet nature, the immense power and beauty of the heart you have access to;

Because you are bereft of evil, you are a consummate architect of joy in the world;

Because you are not greedy, your mind and heart possess every valuable quality;

Because you are forever against oppression and tyranny, you whole being is radiant with pure light;

Because you try to make your imagination pristine, you have greatly strengthened the world of human beings;

Because your word is calculatedly good, your speech is a song for the world;

Because your main language is kindness, you speak each and every tongue;

Because you constantly will and desire goodness for everyone, your senses are utterly sane;

Because you try to embody only virtue you are a true hero or heroine;

Because of all of this, you overflow with Love – and the great cup of Love overflows with your character and personality;

And because you have the manifest courage to be you – your own self – you are Love itself;

And because you have a great heart, you are very blessed!

*Especially for good people – this writing suits your character and personality – with Love and best wishes,*

Wednesday, 23/06/2010, 3.03 p.m.

## **A GOOD LUCK MESSAGE.**

May you, in your darkness, find the radiant light of certitude and Truth to design your thoughts;

May you, when forlorn, find the accompaniment of wisdom, to enable you to make meaningfully rich and appropriate decisions;

May you, when in calamity, find the presence of mind to remain cool, calm, collected and find the patience and Love to guide you;

May you, when your path is blocked, transcend intellectually and find a way to the state of peace;

May you, when poor, find faith, and strength of character to shape your actions and words;

May you, when the tendency to be bitter presents itself as overwhelming, have time to take stock and make the magnificent choice to defer to kindness;

May you, when sorrowing, and in grief, find a suitable wise philosophy, and the consoling words of someone who loves you;

May you, when accomplished, find humility and the human touch;

May you, always, always, in life, find and possess dignity;

May you always retain and reflect Beauty.

>    For you, with best wishes,
>    Shakil A. I. Dawood.

YMm

# Goodness Kindness and Love

# POETRY

# COPYRIGHT

## © SHAKIL A I DAWOOD
## SEPTEMBER 2014

# LONDON

Printed in Great Britain
by Amazon